Women's Ice Hockey Basics

AARON FOESTE

*photography by
Bruce Curtis*

Sterling Publishing Co., Inc.
New York

This book is dedicated to the Brooklyn Blades Ice Hockey Club and to Clint Dahlk, my pee-wee hockey coach in Verona, Wisconsin, who taught—with patience, skill, and humor—both skills and sportsmanship.

Library of Congress Cataloging-in-Publication Data

Foeste, Aaron.
  Women's ice hockey basics / Aaron Foeste ; photography by Bruce Curtis
    p.   cm.
  Includes index.
  ISBN 0-8069-6511-8
  1. Hockey for women. I. Title.
  GV848.6.W65F64   1999
  796.962'082—dc21   99-20769
                                                        CIP

1 3 5 7 9 10 8 6 4 2

Published by Sterling Publishing Company, Inc.
387 Park Avenue South, New York, N.Y. 10016
© 1999 by Aaron Foeste
Distributed in Canada by Sterling Publishing
% Canadian Manda Group, One Atlantic Avenue, Suite 105
Toronto, Ontario, Canada M6K 3E7
Distributed in Great Britain and Europe by Cassell PLC
Wellington House, 125 Strand, London WC2R 0BB, England
Distributed in Australia by Capricorn Link (Australia) Pty Ltd.
P.O. Box 6651, Baulkham Hills, Business Centre, NSW 2153, Australia
Printed in China
All rights reserved

Sterling ISBN 0-8069-6511-8

I would like to thank the following individuals and organizations. Without their help, it would not have been possible to create this book.

The players, coaches, and administrators from the following women's hockey teams: Brooklyn Blades, including Kris Dalton, Caroline Roberts, Lynn Harris, Buena Guzman, Margaret Lillard, and Paula Hunt; New Jersey Colonials, including Donna Guariglia, Sue Collins, Patty Lehrhoff, Steve Carr, Paul Sylvester, Bridget Sylvester, Shannon Sylvester, Colleen Sylvester, Marybeth Mikuski, Loren Oplinger, Meaghan McLaughlin, and Colleen Flynn; Long Island Hurricanes, including Jodie Bard, Lisa Koehler, Wendy Peace, A.J. Sensale, and Ellen Bernhardt; Essex Hunt Club, including Alec and Sally Walsh; Beaver Dam Club, including Virginia Pierrepont; Stuart Country Day School; Beacon Hill Club; and Pelham Pellicans.

Fran Rider and the Ontario Women's Hockey Association; Bob Thornton and Dan Marshall at Ice Works, Syosset, N.Y.; Cory Doyle; Bruce McShane; Canon camera; Kelly Dyer at Louisville Hockey; Suzette Samaroo, fitness expert at Bally Sports Clubs NYC; Marie Allegro, weight-lifting champion, Bally Sports Clubs NYC; Jane and Mutzgar Wittenwyler; the patient and caring Sterling editors Sheila Anne Barry and Hannah Steinmetz; my attorney, Carol Anne Herlihy, Esq.; photographer Bruce Curtis; Paul Driver, at the Brampton Canadettes Tournament; *Hipcheck* magazine and staff; www.whockey.com; and finally, special thanks to Martha Ehrenfeld, her car, my parents, and to anyone else who has ever given me a ride to the rink.

Contents

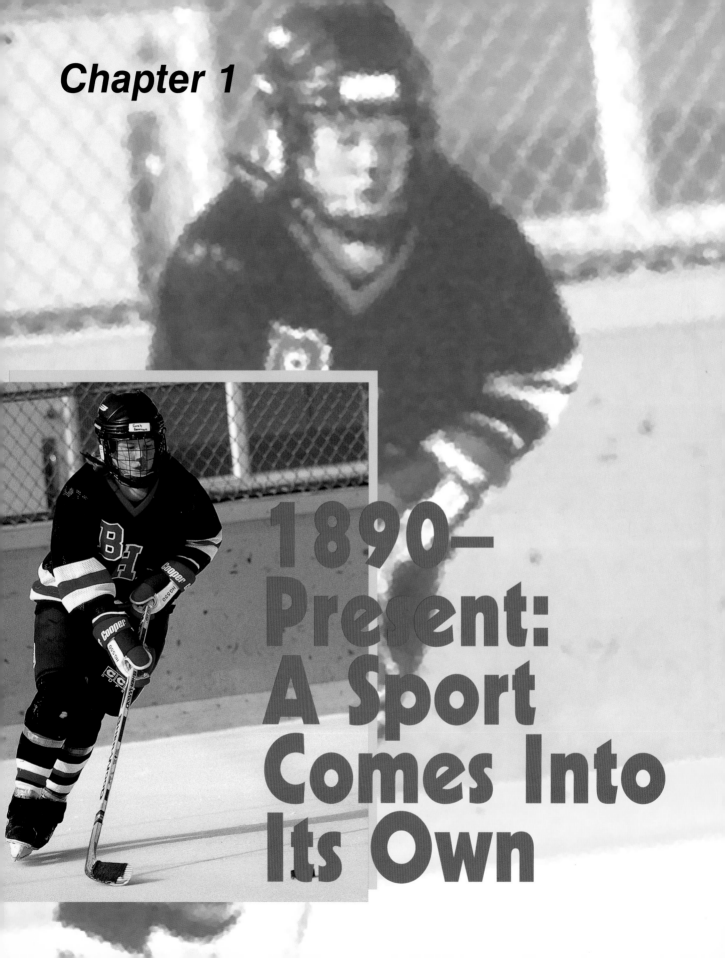

Chapter 1

1890–
Present:
A Sport
Comes Into
Its Own

When women's ice hockey made its 1998 Winter Olympic debut it obviously wasn't the first time women played hockey, but it might as well have been: millions of people saw—for the first time in their lives—very talented female players skating in highly competitive games. After a century of battling, mostly in obscurity, for the right to play hockey, the best female players were now skating in front of the world. To women's hockey enthusiasts, it didn't ultimately matter which team took home the gold medal. The sport itself had finally won the game. After a week in the Olympic spotlight, women's ice hockey had more new fans than the sport had had in its 100-year history.

With very little past exposure for women's hockey, it is no surprise that few people know much about its history. Many of the historical milestones mark important victories in the ongoing battle for equality with male players and men's programs. However, for short periods in the past, women's hockey also enjoyed success and acceptance—and women's teams played in front of crowds of thousands.

Like men's hockey, women's hockey started in Canada. In the 1880s, Lord Stanley (as in *Stanley Cup*) frequently faced off with his daughters on the frozen lawn of Government House in Ontario. In fact, his daughter Isobel is the subject of the earliest photo of a woman playing hockey. It was taken in 1890. Historians consider a game between two women's teams that took place a year later to be the start of women's hockey. When hockey spread south of the border, women were caught up in the excitement as well as men. By 1916 an international tournament was held in Ohio, where U.S. teams competed against Canadian ones.

The sport soon started its other prosperous, albeit short, run at the national level. In the 1920s and 1930s the Edmonton Monarchs, Preston Rivulettes, Black Cats of Haileybury, Toronto Varsity, and Edmonton Rustlers were some of the successful women's teams that barnstormed across Canada. Attendance was in the thousands at their games. Women's hockey briefly took hold and was a success in the world's greatest hockey country.

But the success wouldn't last. When World War II started, and when men's professional hockey started to grow in popularity, women's hockey teams went out of business. At the end of the war, most of the star players hadn't skated for several years, and few players were around to rekindle a sustainable league. Communities began to view hockey as a man's sport and did little to accommodate any new female players. Soon it did not occur to most girls that they could even play ice hockey. The girls who did want to play were often turned away by teams and leagues that were set up for boys only.

In some cases girls did join male teams. In 1955 Abby Hoffman registered to play hockey in Toronto as "Ab" Hoffman. She was one of the league's top players and was selected for the all-star team. Then, when officials checked her birth certificate, they discovered she was a girl! Sadly, from that point on Abby was forbidden to play in the league. She went on to become a swimming and track star, and represented Canada in the 1972 Olympics. Abby's story has become well known, though until recently it was not uncommon for women and girls to hide their female identity when registering for male hockey leagues.

A decade later, in a much less famous case, the organization, not the individual, did the name changing. Nancy Milholland registered for the New York Rangers hockey camp in 1966. Finding it hard to believe that a girl was interested in hockey, they sent their correspondence to "Mr." Nancy Milholland! She chose a different camp and went on to play for the Dartmouth University women's team.

The hockey establishment worked hard to keep women out of the game. Women could break into hockey on an individual

"Mr." Nancy Milholland skates in New York's Central Park in the 1960s.

basis, but there wasn't enough support, or players, to sustain many all-female teams. In the 1998 Olympics it was rare to find a North American player who did not play on a boys' team at some point in her career. Even in the 1970s there were roughly 5,000 registered female players in Canada compared to over 500,000 registered male players.

Women and girls desperately wanted to hit the ice and play a team sport. In Canada the winter can be eight months long, and the culture is centered around life at the local rink. Ringette, a game similar to ice hockey and little known outside Canada, was invented in 1963 as an alternative to ice hockey for girls. The sport is played on skates, players wear pads almost identical to those in hockey, and they use a straight stick to shoot a rubber ring. Precise skating and intricate teamwork are required. Body checking is not allowed.

Hockey would now be for boys, and ringette for girls. The new sport quickly became popular. Canada had close to 15,000 registered ringette players by the early 1980s. Ringette was a great team sport and developed a strong and passionate following. But what about the women and girls who wanted to play ice hockey?

In 1972 U.S. Federal Law, Title IX, was passed. Three years later in Canada, the Ontario Women's Hockey Association (OWHA) was formed. These two events

paved the way for the modern expansion of women's hockey in North America.

The OWHA's goal was to educate, register, and promote female hockey teams and players. It lobbied intensely for a women's national championship, which it first hosted in 1982. Today the organization has over 1,400 registered teams and hosts many prestigious local, national, and international women's tournaments.

Title IX stated that no one could be excluded, based on gender, from any educational program or activity receiving federal financial assistance. Schools and colleges now had to offer men and women equal opportunity in all aspects of education, including sports. Men's hockey had become very popular, and many schools that received federal funds had men's hockey programs. They would have to offer hockey to women or risk losing their funding.

and in 1989 the OWHA eliminated it in all of its games. By doing so women's hockey started down a fresh, skillful path by emphasizing passing, teamwork, and skating. The reduced risk of injury, combined with the success of the 1987 World Tournament, caused registrations to soar.

The rule to eliminate body checking is still occasionally debated in women's hockey circles. Throwing a check can be a highly developed skill and a great defensive tactic. However, the games are still

While parts of society may have been concerned with the rough or "nonfeminine" image of women playing hockey, there is a real risk of injury to women—and men—who compete in the sport. Unfortunately, violence is encouraged in many leagues, and injuries result. Even when the rules are followed, there is a distinct disadvantage for a smaller, lighter player competing against a larger player of equal skill. Women have a greater risk of injury when they compete against men. For men and women, the risk of injury is also greater in a checking game than it is in a nonchecking game.

In 1986 body checking was prohibited in women's national championship games,

very physical without the checking. With player registrations and game attendance at an all-time high, it is clear that the fans and players have responded positively and enthusiastically to the modern game.

The skill level in women's hockey has risen to such a high level that it is no longer necessary for the top female players to skate in men's leagues to be challenged. Elite teams and national training programs have been set up so that gifted players can develop their talents in high-caliber, all-female programs.

Women's hockey is heading in the right direction now. In the last several years Canadian registrations have risen 400 percent. The number of U.S. registrants has surged past 20,000, and there are over 1,000 teams competing in America. The Brampton Canadettes Ladies Dominion Hockey Tournament* is the largest hockey tournament—male or female—in the world. Over 390 women's and girls' teams participate. Some female players also make good money, and have become famous, through hockey. Goaltenders Manon Rhéaume from Canada and Erin Whitten and Kelly Dyer from the United States have all played in professional hockey games. Manon Rhéaume and the 1998 U.S. Olympic team captain, Cammi Granato, became the sport's first two international media stars, and both appear in numerous television and print commercials.

Countless volunteers, players, administrators, and enthusiasts are working hard to make sure that women's hockey keeps its footing and becomes a mainstream sport available to females everywhere. Everyone in the women's hockey community encourages you to get involved and support the players, teams, and the sport, but most important, if you're a woman or girl, we encourage you to play the game. It will be the fastest, most intense, and most exciting sport you try. Guaranteed.

*Information about registering for the Brampton Canadettes tournament can be found in chapter 10, "Women's Hockey Resources."

Chapter 2

Finding or Creating a Team

You are never too young or too old to start playing ice hockey. The sport has been growing rapidly for the last decade and has expanded into the warmer southern regions. This growth has been fueled by adult players and young players alike, both male and female.

Hopefully there is a women's hockey program in your area. Call your local skating rink and ask about instructional skating, hockey clinics, and women's hockey programs. The Internet is also a great source of information about women's hockey.* If you don't currently ice-skate, you should start with some ice-skating lessons before joining a beginners' hockey group.

It is recommended that females play on all-female teams. However, girls younger than 12 could play in boys' programs if no alternatives exist. Physical injury is not a concern for young girls who compete with young boys: the girls are often bigger and stronger than the boys in their age group anyway. Most important, though, everyone should have a positive experience playing hockey. A girl who starts

Players younger than 12 can skate for either girls' or coed teams.

later than some of her male teammates can feel added pressure being a beginner and the only girl on the team. Unlike a boy in a similar situation, she could be led to believe that she is not as skilled because she is a girl, not simply because she is a beginner. Parents should closely

See chapter 10, "Women's Hockey Resources," for sources of information.

monitor the situation if they have a daughter playing in a predominantly male program.

In most areas male leagues incorporate checking into their games once players are about 12 years old. It is recommended that female players over 12 skate on all-female teams. As the players mature from this point on, the size and strength differences between boys and girls become too great for girls to compete in checking leagues without increased risk of injury. If a female team chooses to play a male team, nonchecking rules should always be followed.

It is recommended that you play for an all-female team if you are older than 12.

If your local rink has no women's hockey, you may be just the person your community needs to start a team. A large percentage of women's teams have been started recently by grass-roots organizers, and these individuals are very willing to share advice in a phone call or an E-mail. In fact, in 1994, when I became the hockey director at the rink in Prospect Park in Brooklyn, New York, there was no women's hockey in New York City. Roughly 15 women and girls signed up for our program's—and the city's—first-ever all-female "learn-to-play hockey" clinic that year. Three years later, female participation had grown by 500 percent, and we had just under 100 women and girls playing. Enthusiasm for women's hockey spread throughout the city, and now other all-female teams exist to compete against. Along the way, I turned to countless other women's team organizers for valuable advice and information.

If you accept the challenge and plan to start a team, be prepared for just about any type of reaction, from strong enthusiasm to cold opposition and uncooperativeness. Begin by talking to the rink directors about starting a women's program that you could play in. Maybe they will set up a team if they know ahead of time that players will join. Ask other women whom you meet at open-skating sessions if they would join a team or help form one. Whatever you do, make sure to

Most women's teams have been started by dedicated volunteers.

spread as much enthusiasm as possible. It's much harder to ignore the desires of a group than it is to ignore an individual.

Keep in mind that most rinks operate 20 hours a day as it is, and difficulty adding a new program may be more of a scheduling issue than opposition to women's hockey. It could take a full season to come up with an open ice-slot. I believe that rinks with full schedules should create times for women's teams. Make sure to point out that diversifying makes sense philosophically, but is also great for business. If you are promised an ice-slot for the upcoming season, do as much advertising and promoting as possible in the meantime.

Chapter 3

Basic Skating Skills & Hockey Knowledge

You were probably a hockey fan long before you decided to start playing. You may already have ice-skating experience as well. If not, you've still got time to learn. Everyone should be familiar with the rules of the game and should develop basic skating skills before joining a team or clinic. Acquiring these skills is easy: simply watch hockey games and go ice-skating.

Understanding the following rules and terms is vital for watching and playing the game, as well as communicating with your coach and teammates.

Offensive Zone: The opposing goalie is in the net here. This is the zone where you try to score. It's bordered by the blue line and the end of the rink.

Neutral Zone: The area between the two blue lines.

Defensive Zone: The opposite of "offensive zone." This is the zone that you must defend. Your team's goaltender is in the net here.

The Slot: This is the area that extends a couple of feet to each side of the net and out to about 20 feet in front of it. No lines mark the slot—it simply describes the best area from which to shoot. The

"low slot" is closer to the net than the "high slot."

Breakout: Advancing the puck out of the defensive zone toward the offensive zone.

Off-Sides: You will be off-sides if you cross the blue line and enter your offensive zone before the puck does. The off-sides rule prevents one member of a team from simply waiting by the opposing goalie when most of the action and the puck are at the other end of the rink, thereby forcing a team to advance the puck as a group.

Icing: Icing prevents you from simply shooting the puck down to the offensive end of the rink if you have not crossed the center red line. If the puck crosses both the center red line and the offensive goal line near the end boards without anyone touching it, icing is called. The referee then returns the puck to your defensive zone for a face-off.

The Point(s): Like the slot, the points are not marked on the ice. They are the areas just inside the blue lines where the defensemen usually play when their team is on offense. The defenseman can also be called a "point," as in "pass it to the point" or "cover the point."

SKATING

You don't have to be a great skater to join a clinic or beginners' team: a good instructional program will concentrate heavily on the fundamentals. You just have to know a few basics to get started. In fact, it's often easier to develop more

advanced skating skills at hockey practice, because you'll forget about your fears as you chase the puck and, with all of the equipment on, falling doesn't hurt.

Rental skates are suitable for a session or two, but you will need to purchase your own skates if you're serious about learning. See chapter 4, "Equipment," for advice on fitting and purchasing skates. It's not a good idea to rush out and buy any other hockey equipment before skating a few times and learning what equipment (or what color equipment) your new team requires. A street-hockey stick is a good investment early in your career, though. You can practice stickhandling and shooting a tennis ball when you're not at the rink working on your skating.

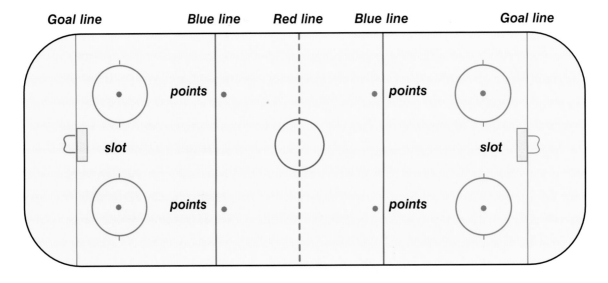

A hockey rink.

Moving: The Duckwalk

When you start, keep your hands on your thighs for better balance.

Turn your toes out like a duck (or a dancer) and take small steps forward. Try to glide between steps. This "duck-walk" turns into the natural skating stride.

If you keep your toes pointed straight ahead you won't go anywhere, and you will look like you're running on a treadmill.

Stopping: The Snowplow

To practice stopping, hold on to the wall, bend your knees . . .

. . . and push one skate sideways against the ice. You should scrape the ice and create a small pile of snow at the end of your push. Pick up your skate to return it to the starting position.

Now push with the other skate. Very little pressure is needed to slide the skate across the ice.

Once you can push your skate across the ice, you're ready to try the "snowplow" stop. Start moving . . .

. . . and glide with both skates on the ice.

Turn one toe inward slightly and push that skate across the ice as you did when you were holding on to the wall. This is called the "one-foot snowplow" and it leads to the more exciting "hockey stop." Try keeping your hands on your knee (of the leg that doesn't push) for balance, and make sure to practice stopping with both the right and left foot.

Turning: The Beginner Turn

Glide with your feet slightly wider than shoulder width.

Turning is easy once you realize a turn is made by simply turning your upper body and head in the direction you want to go.

Make sure to keep your feet wider than shoulder width and your knees bent as you turn your upper body.

You'll stop turning when you stop turning your head, shoulders, and chest. During the turn, your weight will be on your outside skate.

The Swizzle

The swizzle is a very important exercise for developing a strong stride, and it also teaches you to skate backward.

Start with your hands on your thighs, feet together and toes pointed out. Bend at the knees . . .

. . . and push your feet out to the sides.

Now turn your toes in and begin to stand up.

You should end with your feet together and your toes pointed in. This is also the starting position for backward swizzles.

To do a backward swizzle, bend at the knees (as if you were sitting) and, leading with your heels, push your skates out to the sides.

Now turn your heels inward and start to stand up.

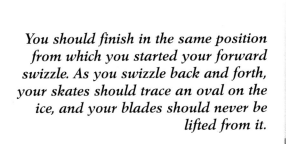

You should finish in the same position from which you started your forward swizzle. As you swizzle back and forth, your skates should trace an oval on the ice, and your blades should never be lifted from it.

Falling Down and Standing Up

Try to recover your balance before you fall by putting your hands on your thighs or toes and bending your knees. If you still have to fall (and you will), tuck your chin to your chest and keep bending until your butt hits the ice.

Never try to stand up from the sitting position. Get on your knees first.

Keep your hands on the ice for balance and get one skate up.

Using your hands and skate, push up onto the other skate and slowly stand up.

Falling isn't so bad. If you remember to bend low before you fall, you won't get hurt.

Chapter 4

Equipment

Your equipment is an integral part of your game: you'll be using it every time you're on the ice, and you must feel comfortable and unhindered in it. Ice hockey requires more equipment than any other major sport. Unfortunately, this adds considerably to the cost of playing. However, it is important not to cut corners when purchasing skates or protective gear.

Always select high-quality equipment that fits properly.* If you're still growing, don't purchase equipment that is too large with the idea that it will last for several seasons: it won't work properly until you do, in fact, grow into it. Equipment comes in women's sizes and models, though the selection is not as vast as it is in men's sizes. Some pieces of equipment designed for men will work just fine for women, while other items, like shoulder pads and pelvic protectors, should be purchased in women's models.

In 1927, female goaltender Elizabeth Graham was on record as the first player ever to wear a face mask. She had adapted a fencing cage for use in her college games. However, over 30 years later, in 1959, Montreal Canadiens goalie Jacques Plante would be officially credited with "inventing" the goaltender's face mask.

SKATES

Skates connect you to the ice and are the tools you use to develop the game's most important skills. They are the most vital

*Please see chapter 7, "The Goaltender," for advice about fitting and purchasing goaltenders' equipment.

pieces of equipment. If you're going to skate two or more times a week, purchase top-of-the-line skates. While they may have enough support when they're new, lower-quality models will not withstand the stress of a competitive season. Many adult women fit into boys' or junior skate sizes. One advantage is the lower cost.

Skates are the most important pieces of equipment.

wear thick socks to fill out skates that are too big (many players don't wear socks at all—they skate barefoot). If you skate in a very cold rink, wearing two pairs of very thin socks will keep your feet warmer. Wearing two pairs of thin socks can also help prevent blisters—the socks rub against each other instead of rubbing against your skin. If you do have blisters or "skate bite," try putting a makeup pad inside your sock at the pressure point (the guys do this too).

Use the following checklist for fitting and caring for skates:

1. Skates should fit your foot "exactly." Because your foot doesn't roll from heel to toe when you skate (as it does when you walk), you don't need space at the end of your toes the way you do in a shoe. Take the foot bed out of the skate and make sure your foot matches it closely.

2. Check for support. The ankle of a good skate should be very stiff. Never purchase a skate if you can squeeze the ankle together.

3. The tongue should be thickly padded to prevent the laces from "biting" into the top of your foot when you bend.

4. Your foot should not slip or roll from side to side inside the skate. If it does, the skate is too wide.

5. Stand or walk around in the store with the skates on for at lease five min-

However, most junior sizes are not designed for the weight and strength of an adult female and can break down quickly. Watch for the introduction of women's skate sizes and models from all the major skate manufacturers.

Getting a good fit in a skate starts with wearing the right kind of sock. Socks should be thin and made of a nonchafing, nonabsorbent, synthetic material. Never

utes before purchasing them. If bothersome pressure points develop, or if the skates become painful within this time, choose another model or size.

6. Used skates are a great way to save money—and a great way to make money if you're selling. Good skates have a lot of life in them. Rarely can a young player break down a pair before they're outgrown. Use the same criteria for selecting used skates as you would for new skates. Just make sure the blade isn't warped, rusted, or sharpened down close to the plastic support. There should be no holes in the inside lining or the outside of the boot. Last of all, don't buy used skates that smell bad.

7. After purchasing skates, make sure to have them sharpened before you leave the store. You'll need to have your skates sharpened after every five to ten sessions on the ice. As a beginner you should ask for a "shallow hollow" when you have your skates sharpened. As you gain more experience, you can experiment with different hollows.

8. Always wipe your blades off when you're finished skating and keep cloth blade guards on them when they're not being used. Cloth guards absorb any water or condensation that remains or forms on the blades, while plastic guards trap moisture that can lead to rusting.

PROTECTIVE GEAR

No matter how expensive or modern a piece of equipment is, it has to feel right or it will slow you down. Good protective gear is lightweight, durable, and very protective. Look at the following photos to see how the equipment is put on and how it should fit.

Suiting Up

Start by putting on your pelvic protector and garter belt. Don't wear sweatpants under your hockey pants— you'll be too hot.

Shin pads go on next.

Hook your socks to your garter belt.

Most pants need to be put on before skates (because the skates won't fit through the legs).

*Your
skates
should be
snug, not
extremely
tight.*

*Position
your shin
pads and
tape them
down
after your
skates
are on.*

*Shoulder
pads are
next . . .*

*. . .
followed
by elbow
pads.*

Jersey . . .

helmet . . .

. . . gloves

. . . ready for action.

*Mouth guards
are a must.*

Tips for Fitting Equipment

Mouth guards: Many players do not understand that a mouth guard can prevent the concussions and broken teeth that result from the lower and upper jaws slamming together during a collision. It is not for preventing the puck from hitting your teeth (that's what the face mask is for). Rinse and store your mouth guard in its own container after each use. Keep a small bottle of mouthwash in your bag for rinsing your mouth guard if you want.

Shin pads: Fit is very important: too big and they'll interfere with your skating; too small and you'll leave areas unpro-

tected against flying pucks and sticks. The bottom of the shin pad should not extend lower than the top lace of your skate, and your knee should be in the middle of the knee cup. Thick padding should wrap around your calf and knee.

Pants: Don't skimp on quality (cost) when it comes to pants, even if you're a beginner. Novices may not need the heavy-duty thigh pads for blocking slap shots, but the padding in the seat that protects you when you fall will be worth the extra money. Pant legs should only overlap slightly with the top of the shin pad, and the top of the pants should

A properly fitted shin pad extends from just above the top lace of your skate to the top of your knee.

extend to cover your kidneys and the bottom sides of your rib cage.

Helmet: Only helmets certified for ice hockey should be used—check the helmet for certification stickers. Most helmets can be adjusted with a screwdriver to fit perfectly. It's your choice to get either a wire face mask or a clear plastic face mask. Some players say the wire cage allows more air to circulate, while others argue that the plastic allows for greater visibility (and it will be easier to see your face if you get your picture in the local paper).

Gloves: Leather will last longer; synthetic is easier to clean. Gloves shouldn't be tight and should be easy to shake off your hands. When you put them on, they

should feel "right" right away. Look for models designed for women—you may shoot and stickhandle better.

Elbow pads: Look for a hard plastic shell and padding that wraps around the forearm and covers the tricep. The elbow pad should not slip or roll on your arm when you move.

Shoulder pads: Women's models are a must for female players. Shoulder pads should not slip or turn on your torso when you move. They should not prevent you from raising your hands above your head (the position you're in after you score).

Equipment Bag: A heavy-duty bag that can take a lot of abuse is a must. Again, a low-quality product probably won't survive more than a season or two.

Throat Protector: A throat protector is made of heavy nylon and fits around your neck like a turtleneck shirt. It is mandatory in many leagues and prevents the throat and neck from being cut or slashed.

Find an equipment bag with a comfortable shoulder strap—it will make a difference after games and on road trips.

The glove, elbow pad, and shoulder pad should form one continuous shield. Any gaps could lead to injuries. Too much overlapping will make movement difficult. A properly cut stick should just reach your chin when you're wearing skates.

You won't be able to weave your way through traffic if your stick is too long.

STICKS

The right stick can make a world of difference in your shot (as will a lot of practice). It's important that you can "flex" the stick when you shoot. Women's models are proportioned around the typical female's hand size and upper-body strength, and most women can flex them better than standard "male" sticks.

Go for a moderate curve and cut the stick so it reaches your chin when you're wearing skates. A good stick feels bal-

anced—the blade should not feel heavy relative to the rest of the stick. Right- or left-handed? Generally, players can't predict whether they will shoot right or left based on the hand they write with. To make this determination, a coach will place a stick on the ground, have the player pick it up, and wait to see how she naturally holds it.

The stick's lie is the angle between the blade and shaft. If you have a bent-over skating style, you'll want to use a #5 lie, or a larger angle between the blade and shaft. If your style is more straight up, go for a smaller angle, or #6 lie. The blade should always be flat on the ice. Too much wear under the heel of the stick indicates a lie that is too big or the stick is too long. Excessive wear under the toe means that the lie is too small or the stick is too short.

Last of all, always tape your stick. Tape will protect the stick and make it last longer. More important, tape improves puck control. The puck is usually spinning and the tape can "grip" and control it.

WASHING YOUR EQUIPMENT

You can and should wash your equipment. One pass by a locker room door will make anyone an advocate of regular equipment-washing. Other than skates, leather gloves, and helmets, all equipment can go in the washing machine or can be hand-washed. It usually gets just as wet when you play and will survive many, many trips through soapy water. Just make sure you rinse it well.

Chapter 5

Power Skating

nce you have mastered the basic skating techniques, it is time to move on to advanced maneuvers. The basic and advanced moves all accomplish the same things: they make you turn, stop, or move. However, the advanced maneuvers in this chapter are much more efficient, take more strength, and can be done at high speeds. Skating expertise is fundamental to hockey. A great skater can do all moves in each direction, so make sure you practice your left and right sides equally. Also, don't underestimate the benefit skating lessons or figure skating classes can have on your game. Look at the definitions in the box below to make sure you understand what is referred to in the descriptions of the exercises.

Inside Edge: the side of the skate blade that faces the other skate

Outside Edge: the side of the skate blade that faces away from the other skate

Inside Leg: when skating in a circle, the leg that is closer to the center of the circle at the beginning of the maneuver

Outside Leg: when skating in a circle, the leg that is farther from the center of the circle at the beginning of the maneuver

THE HOCKEY STOP

The hockey stop is spectacular: the blades dig into the ice, snow shoots into the air, and a player moving at top speed is brought to a stop in less than a second. You should practice the stop while moving slowly at first, and don't worry if you are not spraying ice chips across the ice.

Turn your hips and skates perpendicular to the direction you were traveling (keep your upper body facing the direction you were moving). Push your skates, don't jump, into this position. Slide both blades against the ice as you did in the snowplow stop.

Start moving (slowly at first).

Both blades should be digging into the ice, not just the forward blade. The back foot is on its outside edge and the front foot is on its inside edge.

THE OUTSIDE EDGE TURN

Just as you did in the beginner turn, you must turn your head, chest, and shoulders to make this turn. However, the skates are positioned differently. The right skate leads in a right turn, and the left skate leads in a left turn.

Start moving. Push your lead skate forward (right foot for a right turn).

Turn your head, chest, and shoulders in the direction you want to go.

Keep your lead foot ahead throughout the turn.

Both knees should be bent, and at least half your weight should be on your leading skate.

Your lead foot will be on its outside edge and your back foot on its inside edge naturally: Don't try to lean or dip.

You will continue to turn as long as your upper body is turned.

CROSSOVERS

Crossovers are the best way to accelerate through a turn. In fact, all other types of turns slow you down. If you do them properly, you will be moving much faster after a few crossovers. The following exercises can be done to develop the strength and balance needed to do crossovers. Do these before trying crossovers, and remember, you can't do crossovers while you are moving in a straight line—they are for turning.

Scooter Pushes

Do some scooter pushes to warm up for crossovers. Simply push your way around a circle with your outside foot (as if your inside foot were on a skateboard or scooter). Turn your head, chest, and shoulders toward the center of the circle. It will take several pushes with the outside foot to complete a circle, and your inside skate should never leave the ice.

Stationary Crossovers

Stationary crossovers are a great way to develop the balance necessary to do crossovers. Doing them will teach you to trust that your skate will come down and catch you after you step over the other skate. Look at the following photos.

Start with your feet about shoulder width apart.

Step up and over one skate with the other . . .

. . . and cross your legs. Note that the skate that was stepped over is on its outside edge.

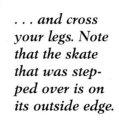

Now, step out from behind and uncross your legs.

You can also practice backward cross-overs. Try walking backward around a small circle by crossing and uncrossing your legs. As you uncross your legs, make sure to swing your hip in the direction of the circle and glide a little with both blades on the ice before crossing again.

Now try a harder crossover exercise. Cross your legs. Then, instead of returning to the starting position, step out from behind and immediately cross your legs the other way without letting your blade touch the ice as you cross. Try this while moving, after you can do it standing still.

Cross your legs.

Step out from behind . . .

. . . and cross your legs again.

Don't let your skate touch the ice until your legs are fully crossed.

Forward Crossovers

Make sure to keep your head, chest, and shoulders turned toward the center of the circle as you do crossovers.

Look at the center of the circle and do a scooter push with your outside leg.

Step your outside skate over your inside skate right after the push.

As your legs cross, push out with your back skate. This is called the "crossunder" push.

Step out from behind to uncross your legs.

Do a scooter push with your outside leg . . .

. . . and step over your inside skate as it pushes.

Step out from behind to uncross your legs.

Remember to keep your upper body turned toward the center of the circle as you do crossovers.

Backward Crossovers

Backward crossovers are similar to forward crossovers: they accelerate you around a corner, and both involve a scooter push and a crossunder push. However, you do not lift your skate off the ice to cross your legs in backward crossovers.

Both blades stay on the ice as the outside skate passes in front of the inside skate. The inside skate is then lifted, or stepped, out from behind to uncross the legs. Imagine your outside skate pushing and your inside skate pulling you around the circle.

Look at the center of your circle and push with your outside leg.

Begin to cross your outside skate in front of your inside skate.

1. Your inside skate should "pull" the ice. This is the cross-under.

2. Step out from behind . . .

3. . . . and return to the starting position.

4. Push with the outside skate . . .

5. . . . as the inside skate pulls and your legs cross.

6. Step out from behind . . .

7. . . . reach for the center of the circle with your inside leg as you uncross . . .

8. . . . and return to the starting position.

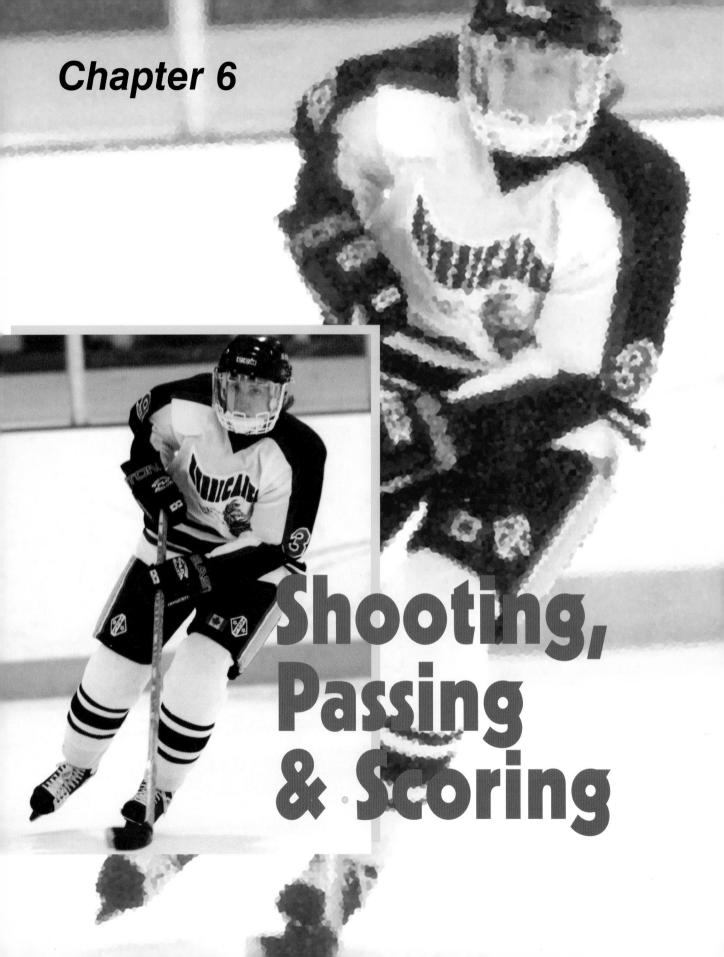

Chapter 6

Shooting, Passing & Scoring

Shooting, passing, and scoring all require keen hand–eye coordination. You must look for a target and then send the puck quickly to it. Don't make the simple mistake of not looking up before you pass or shoot. Good passing and shooting exercises will help you develop the ability to look up and still control the puck. Also you'll develop what hockey players call "soft hands" or "good hands." When you have good hands the puck appears to stick to your blade no matter what you do, and it always hits the mark when you pass or shoot. Being able to catch any pass that comes your way, especially those that aren't right to your stick, is another sign of having good hands.

PASSING

If you haven't heard this before, you will at your first hockey practice: sliding your stick blade back to cushion or absorb the incoming puck is the key to catching passes. If you hold your stick rigidly, the puck is likely to bounce off your blade, just as it bounces off the boards.

To catch a pass you'll first have to give the passer a target—keep your blade on the ice.

Slide your blade back to cushion the incoming puck.

Cushioning the puck prevents it from bouncing off your stick.

To make a pass, look up and use your teammate's stick blade as a target. Keep the puck on your stick as you pass. There shouldn't be a space between your blade and the puck. Space will cause you to slap the puck, when really it should be a smooth, sweeping motion.

After the puck has left your stick, keep moving it . . .

. . . and follow through until your stick is pointing at your target.

A great drill for developing good hands is to pass back and forth with a partner without letting the puck make a sound. To do this, you will need to become an expert at cushioning incoming passes, and you cannot slap the puck as you pass, or you'll hear it hitting your blade. As you and your partner improve, pass harder and see if you can still do it without making any noise. Stand about 10 feet apart for this drill and, as always, make sure to practice your backhand too.

Not every pass will come right to your stick during a game, so don't limit yourself to catching passes with just your stick when you practice. Use your skates to catch pucks that come to your feet. Face your partner and pass the puck into each other's skates. Always catch passes with the sides of your blades. With an inside edge, lightly kick the puck up to your stick and then return the pass. Never try to kick the puck forward with the toe of your blade.

Next, try kicking the puck from your skates back up to your stick while you're moving. Dribbling the puck across the ice using only your feet, like a soccer player, is a great way to develop your footwork.

Kick the puck from your skate to your stick while you are moving.

Practice catching the puck with your skate.

When the puck is shot around the boards, use your skate to catch it. You won't have to turn your back on the rest of the play.

The puck will hit the side of your blade . . .

Stand with your back facing the boards and hold your heel against the wall to catch the puck when it is traveling along the boards.

. . . and be deflected to your stick.

SHOOTING

There are several types of shots, but all have a few things in common. First of all, always follow through with your stick so it points at the target when you shoot. Follow through high to shoot high.

Second, in all shots the weight is transferred from your back foot to your front foot as you shoot. Shooting off the back foot, or not transferring your weight as you shoot, will slow down your shot.

Always transfer your weight to your front foot and follow through so your stick points at the target when you shoot.

The Backhand Shot

When he was a kid, Wayne Gretzky asked Gordie Howe if he had any advice to offer a budding hockey star. Gordie told him to practice his backhand shot. He did, and the rest is history. This shot is one of the most essential but most overlooked shots.

Start with your weight on your back foot. Keep your stick on the puck; don't slap it.

Push down with your top hand and pull up with your bottom hand as you shoot.

As you pull through, transfer the weight to your front foot.

Follow through with your stick pointed at the target.

The Wrist Shot

The wrist shot is like a hard pass: Your stick doesn't slap the puck. Start with the puck behind you and your weight on your back foot. Make sure to look at your target.

Snap your wrists and transfer your weight to your front foot as you shoot.

All the weight is transferred to the front foot, and the back foot ends up off the ice in a hard wrist shot.

The Snap Shot

The snap shot is a quick shot used to surprise goalies or when you don't have time for a longer setup. Look up at your target . . .

. . . and take a quick shot by snapping your wrists.

The Slap Shot

You might be making two common mistakes when you practice your slap shot. The first is, you shouldn't be practicing it yet. The slap shot integrates the timing and skill of the other shots, and you need to have good wrist and snap shots to get it. By perfecting the other shots, you'll improve your slap shot. Second, don't face the net (with your body) when you take a slap shot. For the shot to work, you need to have your shoulder or side angled toward the net.

The puck should be in front of you in the space between your feet. Wind up . . .

. . . and slap the ice just behind the puck. Notice how the stick flexes from hitting the ice. Snap your wrists as you make contact with the puck.

Follow through. All the weight ends up on the front foot, and the back foot is off the ice in the slap shot.

The Off-Season

To develop a great shot, you will need to practice outside the rink as well.

It will take a lot more than just attending your team's practices to develop a good shot. See chapter 9, "Training and Crosstraining," for off-season shooting tips and strength exercises.

SCORING

When you shift your attention from the goalie to the net, you'll see that the corners of the net are the best places to shoot for. It's not necessary to lift the puck to score. The hardest corner for the goalie to defend is the corner on the ice on her stick side. Think about it this way: If you had to catch a speeding puck, would you rather do it with your hand or with your foot? The goalie can play high

shots with her hands. Any shot on the ice on her stick side must be blocked with her skate, which is slower than using either of her hands. The least favorable corner to shoot for is above her catching glove. The glove is designed for snagging pucks from the air and moves quickly compared to the legs.

Look at the picture above. Do you see a goalie staring at you? Or do you see all the open corners in the net behind the goalie? Don't make the mistake of focusing on the goalie before you shoot. Train yourself to look for the net in back of the goalie instead. Locate the open spot where you want your shot to go.

Shoot when you have the chance.

Just about every goal is preceded by a shot. That might seem pretty obvious, but during a typical game it looks like players don't all understand this. If you're not scoring as much as you want to (or should be), there might be a simple reason: You don't recognize a good opportunity to shoot the puck. It's not necessary to skate around all the defensemen before you shoot. Simply move toward the slot and fire the puck. The more shots you take, the more goals you will score. When you try to move from a good shooting position to an "even better" one, the puck is usually lost and no shot is taken.

Moving the Goalie

When you make the goalie move, you increase your chances of scoring. Instead of skating straight at the net, skate across the area in front of the net. As you move from one side to the other (even 20 feet away from the net), the goalie has to move from one side of the net to the other to stay in position to block your shot. As the goalie moves through the center of the net, the corners "open up" and it is easier to score.

You can also move the goalie by passing to a teammate on the other side of the net. Again, the goalie has to move from one side to the other to cover the shot. If you pass fast enough, you can catch the goalie out of position and score.

Playing the Off Wing and Cutting to the Middle

Skating down the wing, cutting to the middle, and shooting is one of the best ways to score. When you cut, you change direction. You are no longer skating toward the net, you are now skating parallel to it. This makes the goalie move. She can no longer stay in position by simply keeping her leg planted against the side of the net.

Second, when you change direction the defenseman who is keeping you in check must change direction as well. It will take her a moment to react. During this time, she will still be moving backward while you head toward the middle. A space for seeing the net and setting up a quick shot opens up between you and the defenseman right after you cut. If you wait too long she will catch up to you.

If you are a right-handed shot and you are skating on the left wing, you are playing the "off wing." For a left-handed shooter, this means playing on the right side. Playing the off wing is important for taking quick shots after you cut. A right-handed player who cuts from the left side is immediately in position to take a shot. However, if the same player were to cut to the middle from the right side, she would be in position to take a backhand shot, not a forehand shot. Practice skating down the off wing, cutting, and shooting until it becomes a smooth, natural motion.

To score more goals, create shooting opportunities out of average situations. Don't wait for a breakaway or try to skate the puck too far into the zone. Shoot between the defenseman's legs or under her stick. Aim your shots to go just past the side of her leg. She will screen the goalie's view of the puck for you. Instead of trying to beat the defenseman, you will be using her to help you score.

Cut toward the center from the off wing and take a hard shot right away.

Chapter 7

The Goaltender

It is not the goaltender's equipment that most sets her apart from her teammates: it's her state of mind. Playing this position is a mental, as well as physical, challenge. In the game statistics, it is the goaltender who is designated as having "won" or "lost" each game for her team. She must have the emotional resources to deal with this tremendous pressure. She also must have the mental stamina to concentrate on the puck for the entire game, rather than only one shift at a time.

The position also demands great skating and athletic ability. Lightning-quick reflexes are required to snare pucks from the air. She relies on complicated footwork and skating expertise to outmaneuver a fast-skating forward. Don't take up goaltending if you're looking for a refuge from skating drills or conditioning. Goaltenders can skate with the best forwards, and must be very physically fit to play the entire game while wearing over 25 pounds (10 kg) of equipment.

Goaltenders have a vocabulary, training exercises, and maneuvers that are unique to them. Unless you're very fortunate, your team's coach may not know a lot of the position's finer points. Specialized training camps, staffed by goalie coaches and ex-goaltenders, are a great way to learn the advanced techniques. There you'll be taught strategies for the mental aspects of the game as well as the physical, and you'll experience the camaraderie of other goaltenders, possibly for the first time.

EQUIPMENT

The idea behind playing goalie is to get hit with the puck, so clearly you should not skimp when purchasing protective gear. Unfortunately, the gear is much more expensive than the equipment the other skaters use. If you want to save money, try to find used equipment until you've stopped growing.

Suiting Up

A goaltender's equipment bag is huge.

A goalie wears a pelvic protector, garter belt, and socks, just like her teammates.

Knee pads are put on next. These protect the parts of the knees that are exposed after you've dropped to the ice to make a save.

Specialized goaltender's pants, which are shorter and have a lot more padding than regular pants, are put on next.

Goalie skates have flat blades, short cuffs, and a hard protective shell.

Optional ankle guards can be worn over the skates.

The massive leg pads are first strapped to the skate . . .

. . . the calf, and the thigh.

Now put on the chest/arm/shoulder unit.

Goalie jerseys are extra-wide and have short arms, but even they can be a tight squeeze.

Put your helmet on next. A goaltender's throat/neck protector should also be worn. All that is needed now is the catching and blocking gloves, and the stick.

Time to hit the ice.

THE STANCE

Good balance and a proper stance are the fundamentals upon which all the other maneuvers are built. Keep your head up, knees bent, weight over the balls of your feet, blades on their inside edges, and lean your upper body forward slightly. Your catching glove should be held up and open. Keep your stick on the ice a few inches in front of your skates and leg pads. Your body should always be square to the puck.

MOVEMENT: GOING POST TO POST

When the puck is in the corner, plant the entire

side of your body and your skate against the post. The puck is only one inch by three inches (2.5 by 7.5 cm); any gaps could allow the puck to sneak in, resulting in an easy goal. Also, from this position you can use your stick to check opponents as they skate behind your net.

The Shuffle

Push with your right skate to "shuffle" to the left across the net.

Keep your toes pointed forward and your body square to the puck.

As you push with the right, the left slides against the ice as it does in a hockey stop.

The T-Push

The T-push is a faster way to move across the net. It is used if you have to go from one post to the other at once.

Turn the toe of the leading skate toward the far post. The toe of the pushing skate faces forward. In this position your feet make a "T."

MOVEMENT: FORWARD AND BACKWARD

Move out to the top of the crease to cut down the angle when the puck is in front of you. Back up to the post when the puck is in the corner. As the shooter approaches on a breakaway, back up so she can't make a move around you. To understand what the shooter sees, look at an object in the distance. Hold a finger up and move it closer and farther from your eye as you continue to look at the object. When your finger is close to your eye, it blocks more of your view. Similarly, when you move forward (closer to the shooter), it blocks some of her view of the net and cuts down the angle for her shot.

Come out of the net to cut down the angle.

SEEING THE PUCK

Do whatever you have to do—bend, squat, lean—to keep your eye on the puck. Try bending lower and looking through the legs of the players in front of you.

Look through the net to see the puck when it is behind you. Only turn your head—never your body—to look behind the net. Remember to always keep your leg planted against the post when the puck is behind the net or in the corner.

CONTROLLING THE PUCK

Covering the Puck

Goaltenders are allowed to cover the puck to stop play. Always cover the puck when the opposition is close. Pay attention to the flow of the game. If your team needs to change lines, try to cover the puck. However, if your team is on a power play and the opposing players are not putting on much pressure, keep the puck in play.

Drop on a loose puck if the opposing players are close.

Cover the puck with your body and stick, so that it cannot be poked free before the whistle blows.

Passing the Puck

Participate in passing drills during your team's practices so you can pass the puck to teammates during a game.

MAKING SAVES

A good goalie can stop the first shot, but it takes a great goalie to stop the second in a series. Deflect shots into the corners away from your net so your opponent can't shoot the rebounded puck. Don't hold your

Don't go down to stop an easy shot.

stick against your leg pads or toes. The stick won't "give," and a lot of rebounds will bounce off it as a result. Whether or not you can stop the second shot depends on how quickly you get up after going down to make the first save. Don't go down for shots you could stop standing up.

THE MENTAL GAME

Do a basic warm-up and prepare mentally in the locker room before the game.

After a goal is scored, take a second to determine how you could have made the save and then don't think about it again during the game. You must prepare yourself for the next shot, not the last one.

Concentrate on the puck and the movement of the players wherever they are on the ice.

Chapter 8

Playing Without the Puck

Your team should follow a planned system for covering the opposing players and regaining the puck when you don't have possession of it. Your team will also need a system to control and keep the puck when you are on the offense. In recreational leagues a simple plan can have dramatic results. At higher levels, an unorganized team will provide little challenge to a well-coached group that moves the puck fluidly between its players. Defensively, the superior team can even direct where the weaker team chooses to take the puck.

Hockey is a fast and dynamic game. The distinction between offense and defense is not as clear-cut as it is in other sports. A team can change from offense to defense and back in a matter of seconds at any spot on the ice. When the puck is loose, you must make a split-second decision as to which team is more likely to recover it. Experienced players can react accordingly and be in either a defensive or offensive position when the puck is recovered.

As the puck and the other players move about, your responsibilities will shift from one area to the next, and from one opposing player to the next. Even if you don't handle the puck during a shift, you should return to the bench winded from sprinting to be in forechecking, backchecking, or breakout plays. Never underestimate the

Hustle to be in the right position when you don't have the puck.

value of being in the right position. You may prevent a scoring chance for an opponent, or you could cause her to make a bad pass that results in a goal for your team. Again, you can accomplish this without touching the puck.

To play well without the puck, you must recognize and anticipate the actions of your opponent. Imagine how you would feel and react in her situation. Take advantage of the quick decisions you force her to make. Anticipate and react to where she is going to pass, not where she has passed. Don't hold back. Only the most experienced players stay calm under pressure—and even they make mistakes. By pressuring the puck carrier and her teamates, you and your teammates can control the movement of the puck.

FORECHECKING

Once the puck has been shot into the corner or behind the net in your offensive zone, your team should try to trap it there and regain possession of the puck. Note what the opposing players are doing, especially the defenseman who must retrieve the puck, and you will immediately know how to best trap the puck in your zone.

If the opposing defenseman is skating back to pick up the puck, you will see the back of her jersey as you enter the zone. Because she is not facing forward, she has not been able to assess her passing options or to see where you and your teammates are positioned. In this situation you will use a forechecking system

This defenseman has picked up the puck from behind her net and is advancing it forward (you see the front—not the back—of her jersey). She has seen where her teammates are, so you should assume she will complete a pass. Your goal is to trap the player who receives her pass.

that makes her rush and places your teammates in positions to intercept her pass. However, if you see her advancing the puck forward, she has had the chance to look at her passing outlets, and you must use a system to trap the player to whom she passes.

The following diagrams show a

forechecking system for each situation (among the many systems you can use). In each diagram the opposing players are represented by an "X." You and your teammates are F1, F2, F3, D1, D2 (meaning "first forward," "second forward," "first defenseman," etc.). A lowercase "p" is used to symbolize the puck.

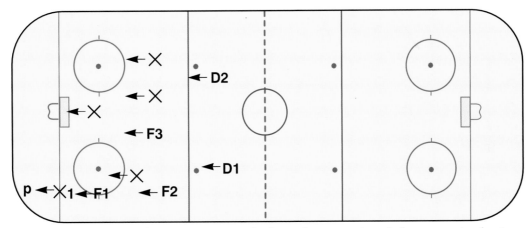

The Corner Trap: This system is used when the opposing defenseman is skating into the corner to get the puck. F1 pressures X1, hoping she will make a blind pass that can be intercepted by F2 or F3. Her only option is to send the puck behind the net. F1 is always the first forward into the zone. It does not matter if F1 is one of the wings or the center.

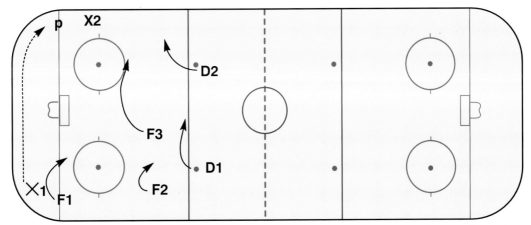

The Corner Trap: Often X1 will panic under pressure and shoot the puck up the near boards to F2. If X1 shoots the puck behind the net (her only real option under pressure), be prepared to react and transition quickly to trap the puck on the far side.

Quickly determining who F1, F2, and F3 are is as simple as looking at the jersey of the opposing defenseman. If you don't see any of your teammates ahead of you, you're F1. Likewise, if you see a linemate chasing the puck carrier into the corner, you're F2, and so on.

The Wedge

The puck is dumped deep inside your offensive zone. You see that the opposing defenseman has possession of the puck, is set up behind her net, and is deciding where to pass. Assume she will complete one pass. Forecheck in a manner that forces her to pass to one side—the side where you and your teammates are planning to trap the puck. The "Wedge" is a good system to use in this situation. In all forechecking systems, F1 must take charge and force the opponent into making quick decisions. Then F1's teammates can take advantage of the opponent's mistakes.

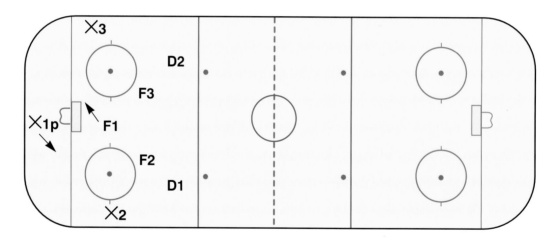

When the forechecking team attacks in the "V"-shaped wedge, X1 has no passing options other than a very wide pass to either side. F1 must flush X1 from behind the net: As soon as F1 moves in one direction toward the side of the net, X1 will skate out from the other side..

Forechecking Tip: Skate with your stick on the ice and toward the center of the rink to take away the cross-ice passing lane.

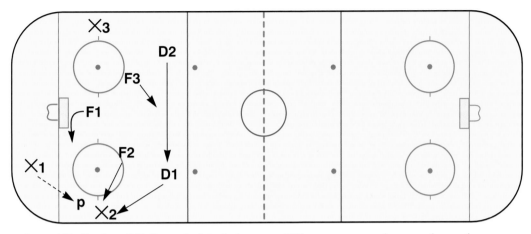

Once F1 flushes X1 from behind the net, F1's teammates know where the pass has to go and can move to trap the puck on that side.

The Neutral Zone Trap

This trap can be used when the opposition is advancing the puck and can't be trapped deep. After dumping and changing, your forwards will not have time to skate far into the offensive zone, so you should set up your forechecking system in the neutral zone. Teams can also use this system late in the game to protect a lead: there is less risk of the other team having a two-on-one or a breakaway.

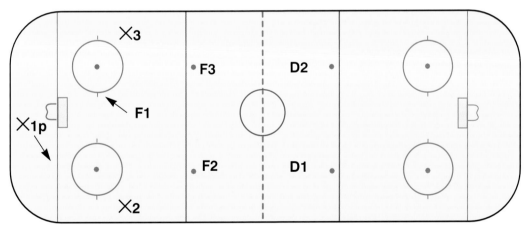

Like the other forechecking systems, the Neutral Zone Trap forces the opposition to pass wide where the puck can be trapped against the boards.

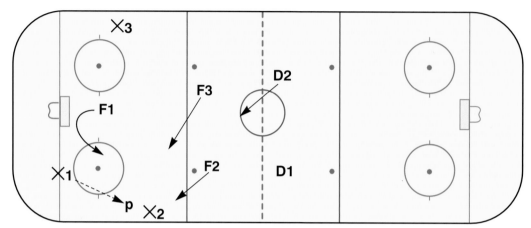

As F1's teammates move to close the trap, all passing lanes are blocked and the opposition's forward progress is shut down.

BACKCHECKING

If you're a forward, try not to think of your defensemen as the players who are responsible for breaking up every play by the opposition. Those are your duties as well. Overtake the puck carrier and other players from behind, and stop the shot or pass before your defensemen are forced

Knock the puck away from the opposing player before she reaches your defensemen.

to commit. Even if you can't catch the puck carrier, chase hard after her. If your defenseman collides with her, the very next player on the scene will gain possession of the loose puck: this player should be you—not a forward from the other team.

Backchecking may require you to take your eyes off the puck and focus on the other team's forwards, who are good passing outlets. Follow and cover an open forward, much as you would in basketball, to prevent her from receiving a pass, picking up a loose puck, or shooting a rebound. By aggressively covering the forward on your side of the ice, you allow your teammates to concentrate fully on regaining possession of the puck from the puck carrier.

When possible, backcheck at an angle that forces the puck carrier toward the boards. Checking is not permitted in women's hockey. However, physical contact is allowed and is an integral part of the game. The contact must occur as a result of your attempt to reach the puck. You are not allowed to block a player's movement or to run into her while making no effort to play the puck.

Physical contact can occur as you try to get the puck, but you cannot check her into the boards.

Backcheck from an angle that forces the puck carrier toward the wall.

PLAYING DEFENSE

When playing defense, concentrate on the opposing player's torso or jersey. The puck, her eyes, and her head can be used to deceive you. However, a skilled forward cannot skate out of her own jersey. Watch the logo on an approaching forward's jersey, not her eyes or the puck. She, her jersey, and the logo travel as one. When you focus on the logo, you will know where she is headed.

Focus on the open player, not the puck, in front of your net.

Use your stick to try to regain the puck or to check her stick. You cannot use your stick to hit or block her body.

Your biggest responsibility in front of your own net is to keep an opposing player's stick off the ice. If you are facing the puck when it is in the corner, a player can move behind you, quickly receive a pass, and shoot the puck into your net. Face the player, not the puck, and keep her stick up so she cannot receive a pass or take a shot.

Defensive Zone Coverage

In this system, the wings' responsibilities are the points and the high slot; the center's responsibilities are the corners and the low slot. Each defenseman works in front of the net and in the corner on her side. When the puck moves from one side of the ice to the other, you and your teammates should shift quickly and fluidly from one responsibility to the other so that no area is left uncovered.

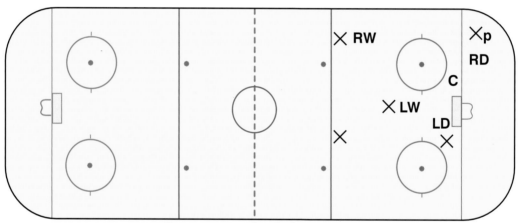

Setting up in the defensive zone.

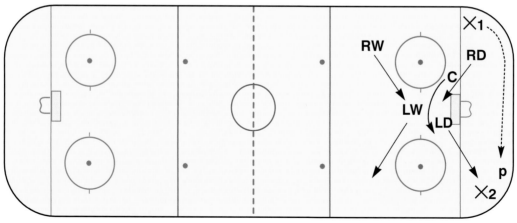

Note how the players shift when the puck moves from one side of the ice to the other.

Shift quickly when the puck moves to the other side of the ice.

Always keep one defenseman in front of the net. The other defenseman's job is to dig the puck out of the corner or from behind the net. When the puck is shot from the left corner to the right corner, the defensemen shift: the right defenseman leaves the slot and skates to the right corner to get the puck, and the left defenseman leaves the left corner and covers the slot. The wing covers the point when the puck is on her side of the ice. When it is on the opposite side, she should cover the high slot. The center works with the defensemen in front of the net and in the corners.

There is a fine line between offense and defense. During the breakout, your team is on offense even though you're in your defensive zone. When you see that a teammate will recover a loose puck, anticipate an offensive pass and hurry to get in position to receive it. When it's not clear who will recover a loose puck, keep covering your player until you see who gets it.

KILLING PENALTIES

There are two basic formations typically used to kill penalties. Again, remember that you can cause your opponent to make mistakes by pressuring her. Don't give the power-play unit too much time to make a perfect pass. When you have four players on the ice, think of the forwards as "right" and "left" forwards as opposed to wings or a center and a wing.

The Box

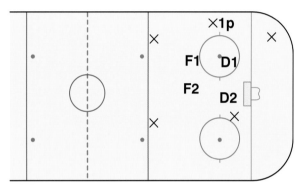

The typical setup for four players is called the "box."

The Triangle

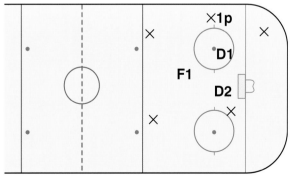

Use the "triangle" when two players have to sit out.

Chapter 9

Training &
Crosstraining

n a game, a typical player will probably not shoot more than four times or play for more than 15 minutes. Clearly, practices—not games—are the times to work on skills and physical conditioning. However, just attending your team's practices will not be enough to develop and maintain the skills necessary to play at a competitive level. Fortunately, you can make a lot of improvements during your own training sessions. Determine what aspect of your game needs the most work so that you can train appropriately and efficiently to reach your goals. Do your shooting skills need more work than your skating skills? Weight lifting will improve your strength and shot. Are you out of shape? In-line skating is great for conditioning and improving your skating. Also, attending a summer hockey camp is much more helpful than playing extra games if you need to work on the basics.

It doesn't matter how skillful you are if you are in poor shape physically. Physical conditioning is as fundamental to hockey as skating is. Concentrating and performing are nearly impossible when you're tired. Also, conditioning and skill development go hand in hand: if you can't beat the opposition to the puck because you're exhausted, you won't get many chances to shoot or stickhandle. A lesser-skilled but better-conditioned team can usually compete successfully against a more

Note: Most of the information and exercises in this chapter are for players over the age of 14. Younger players should concentrate on skill development, not strength training and conditioning. If you're under 14 years of age, your regular hockey practices and other activities are more than enough to keep you in great playing condition. Also, strenuous weight lifting and conditioning exercises can cause injuries if you're still growing. Every player should check with her physician before starting a training program.

highly skilled, poorly conditioned team. The same goes for individual players. Use conditioning as one of your weapons, just as you would your shot or favorite move.

There are many off-ice activities that improve both hockey skills and physical fitness. The best training programs combine skill development and conditioning, and your coaches probably run on-ice drills that work on both simultaneously. Try to structure your own training program in the same manner. Combine fun hockey-related activities with conditioning exercises, and work out with teammates or friends if you want.

CARDIOVASCULAR CONDITIONING

When training for hockey, you'll need to work on power, strength, and endurance. A long, moderately paced bike ride, run, or skate are examples of aerobic (endurance) workouts. Power and strength—or anaerobic training—will improve your performance during each shift, when you need quick bursts of speed and strength. Sprinting and weight lifting are examples of anaerobic exercises.

"Aerobic" simply means "with oxygen." Your muscles use oxygen to convert carbohydrate (sugar), fat, or protein to energy. "Anaerobic" means "without oxygen." Your muscles can also burn one fuel—sugar— without oxygen. When you work at over

90 percent of your total capability (during a sprint, for example), enough oxygen can't be supplied to generate the great amount of energy needed. That's when your anaerobic system kicks in to supply the rest of the energy by breaking down sugar quickly. Lactic acid is left behind as a waste product and causes a burning sensation and soreness.

Your cardiovascular system consists of your heart, lungs, arteries, veins, and capillaries and is the oxygen delivery/waste pickup system for working muscles. It becomes stronger and more efficient with regular exercise. Even though fat is a great fuel source, converting it to energy is more complicated than converting sugar to energy. As your muscles and aerobic system become well trained, a greater percentage of fat will be burned. By exercising the anaerobic system you will be able to sustain an intense pace for longer periods, produce more power, and develop the ability to tolerate and remove lactic acid from your muscles.

Balancing anaerobic and aerobic conditioning is important if you're a hockey player. If you only trained your anaerobic system, you'd have three great shifts and then die (not literally). Likewise, if you only developed your aerobic capability, you'd have the endurance to play the entire game, but would have a difficult time outsprinting players to the puck and muscling your way out of the corner.

IN-LINE SKATING

There is no better form of exercise than in-line skating. It always comes out on top when scientists compare different exercises. In-line skating burns calories, builds muscle, strengthens the cardiovascular system, improves coordination, and increases flexibility. It is fun and takes place outdoors. Skating is also a low-impact sport that does not cause long-term, stress-related injuries. In fact, many joggers who have developed knee or foot problems can in-line skate without the stress and pain they experience while running.

Ice hockey players can't ignore another great, tangible aspect of in-line skating: It's basically the same as ice-skating, and skills in one translate almost directly to the other. In-line skates have turned the world into one giant hockey rink. Now players can practice just about anytime and anywhere. Through in-line skating you can improve your skating and conditioning simultaneously, instead of just logging more time on an exercise machine.

Again, like skating skills, any strength and endurance you develop on wheels will translate directly to the ice. Distance skating is an aerobic workout and a great way to develop endurance. Short sprints up hills will develop power.

A few things are not the same on wheels as they are on the ice. Stopping is one major difference. Also, you've never encountered hills or bumps (hopefully) at the ice-skating rink. Take a lesson with a pro or get an in-line skating book so you can catch up on these skills. Once you get

In-line skating is a natural crosstraining exercise for ice hockey.

used to the new stop and to rolling over bumps, everything else—forward crossovers, backward crossovers, turns, etc.—is the same. As in ice hockey, proper equipment is a must for in-line skating. Knee pads, elbow pads, wrist guards, and a helmet should always be worn. If you're serious about training on in-line skates, set up a workout plan for yourself. The following in-line workouts are derived from those done for years by speedskaters.

WORKOUT 1: INTERVALS

Intensity: high

Emphasis: builds muscle, speed, strength, and power; increases anaerobic potential

An interval workout involves skating at a good workout pace of about 60–70 percent of your maximum capability punctuated by intervals of skating at over 90 percent of your total capability. At 90 percent you should feel that you are just short of an all-out sprint. Intervals can be measured on a stopwatch and should be between 20 and 30 seconds long. Convenient landmarks can also be used to mark interval distances if you do not have a stopwatch.

Intervals build muscle, speed, strength, and power—all essential for ice hockey. The short bursts of speed have the same effect as working with weights, and intervals are a great way to work muscles anaerobically. You will feel a burning sensation in your legs as you sprint, and your system will become more efficient at tolerating and removing lactic acid.

The Interval Workout:

➤ Skate at 60–70 percent of capacity for 10 minutes.

➤ Skate at 90 percent for 30 seconds.

➤ Return to 60–70 percent for 1 minute.

➤ Skate at 90 percent for 30 seconds.

➤ Return to 60–70 percent for 1½ minutes.

➤ Skate at 90 percent for 30 seconds.

➤ Return to 60–70 percent for 2 minutes.

➤ Repeat intervals one or two more times.

➤ Skate 5 minutes at 60–70 percent.

➤ Skate slowly for 5 minutes.

➤ Stretch.

Intervals, or any hard skating work, should be done on flat surfaces or up small hills. Glide and catch your breath when you go down a hill. Shorten the time between intervals and increase the length of the interval as you improve.

WORKOUT II: THE ALL-AEROBIC WORKOUT

Intensity: medium

Emphasis: sustained aerobic work, weight loss, and efficient calorie consumption

This workout stresses efficient aerobic metabolism: it is ideal for those who want to lose weight. During steady skating your body begins to burn calories efficiently as it becomes accustomed to the work. Exercising at medium intensity for the right amount of time ensures that muscles do not have to work anaerobically.

Maintain a steady pace of 50–60 percent of maximum speed for a set period of 30 minutes or longer. The workout should be done on the flattest possible route. Talk to your physician about your heart rate. You can then check your heart rate at the beginning, during, and at the end of the workout to make sure that you are in the proper range for a medium-intensity aerobic workout.

WORKOUT III: THE HILL

Intensity: high

Emphasis: strength, power, anaerobic conditioning

The hill workout has almost the same effect on your legs as a hard weight-lifting workout. Find a steep hill whose top takes you between 30 seconds and 2 minutes to reach when you're skating hard. After a 10-to-15-minute warm-up skate, you're going to sprint up the hill, glide back down, and do it all over again! This is a great workout because you can easily keep track of how many times you sprint up the hill. As you get stronger you can increase the number of trips to the top, and as you become familiar with the workout, you can set a goal of skating up the hill a certain number of times. A couple of tips: Don't glide back down the hill if your legs are really burning or are shaky—you don't want to have an accident. Also, you'll probably want to take a water bottle with you and leave it at the bottom or top.

WEIGHT TRAINING

Hockey is a game of speed *and* strength. You have to move opposing players away from your net, and you have to push your way out of the corners. Also, you've got to carry your head and shoulders up, stickhandle, and shoot. Improved upper-body strength can lead to a faster shot. Arm and shoulder strength will also help you skate longer and harder. There is a

Upper- and lower-body strength is very important.

strong arm motion involved in the skating stride: a strong upper body will help pull you along and keep your momentum going.

The best way to develop strength is through weight training. Fortunately, many skating workouts, like skating up hills on in-line skates or sprinting during hockey practice, have a similar effect on your legs as does weight lifting. If you don't have a lot of time and are already doing hard skating work, you can focus on your upper body in the weight room.

Some women are worried about becoming too big or muscular through weight training. This concern is usually based on popular myths. You could never look like a bodybuilder after lifting weights for only a couple of hours each week. Rather, you would have to devote hours a day to developing your muscles.

Second, weight lifting is a great way to lose fat and become slimmer. Muscle tissue consumes energy (calories) 24 hours a day during regular metabolism. More muscle means more calories burned, not to mention that weight lifting is a great calorie-burner itself. Muscle tissue is much more dense than fat. Think of fat as a pillow and muscle as a hardcover book. They weigh about the same, but the book takes up a lot less room and is much firmer. If you "replace" fat weight with muscle weight, your overall weight won't change but you may be a size smaller.

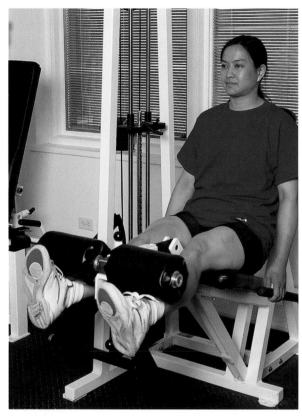

Weight training is a great way to develop strength.

Everyone's body is different, and you can tailor your workout to your specific goals.

One fun aspect of weight training is that the same exercise can usually be done many ways and with several different pieces of equipment. You can use modern equipment at a gym, simple dumbbells and free weights, or no equipment at all (by doing push-ups, pull-ups, etc.). Don't fall into a boring routine; incorporate different exercises regularly and work out in different places. Plan on

having an experienced trainer show you the proper technique for using the equipment if you go to a gym.

It is a general rule in weight training to do exercises that use the most (or the largest) muscle groups first. That way you will do the work that requires the most power and strength first—when you have it. Push-ups or bench presses should be done first in an upper-body workout, and squats or leg presses should be done first in a leg workout. Also, try not to do two groups of exercises in a row that work similar muscles. Triceps are heavily involved in push-ups, so you'll want to do an exercise that doesn't focus on your triceps between push-ups and another tricep exercise.

As with in-line skating, how hard you push yourself during your workout will determine whether or not you're working anaerobically. Many repetitions with a light weight will work your aerobic system only. However, if you choose a weight that you can only lift five times, you can bet that by the fourth or fifth repetition your anaerobic system will be working as well.

There are a few terms you should know before you start. Every time you do a push-up or move a weight it is called a "repetition," or "rep" for short. Groups of reps are called "sets." A good hockey workout will, of course, involve both anaerobic and aerobic work. Pick a weight that allows you to do 10 reps. If after the tenth repetition, you could do five more, the weight is too light. Likewise, if you can barely finish the ninth and can't do the tenth, it's probably too heavy. Do three sets of 10 repetitions of each exercise (for a total of 30 repetitions each). Rest for one minute—not longer—between sets. Last, you can make quick advances in weight lifting. As you improve, make sure to increase the amount of weight you use in order to keep your workouts challenging.

The following photos show some important exercises. You may want to do other routines as well, and you can also have a trainer show you how to do these with different equipment. For a good anaerobic/aerobic balance, do three sets of 10 reps each with a one-minute break between sets, increasing the weight slightly with each set, if possible.

Beginner Push-ups

Lie flat on the floor with your hands just to the sides of your shoulders.

Using your knees for balance, push up until your arms are straight. Make sure you come back down under control.

Regular Push-ups

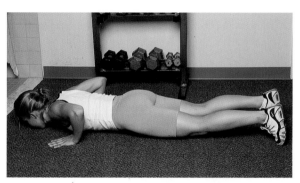

These are done exactly the same as beginner push-ups except . . .

. . . you use your feet, not your knees, for balance. These take more strength than beginner push-ups. Don't arch your back when you do push-ups.

Biceps Curls

Hold two dumbbells. "Curl" one up to your shoulder. The only movement should be from below the elbow—don't swing your arm forward (from the shoulder).

Alternate arms. Make sure to hold your arms close to your sides. Do 10 reps per arm, not 10 reps total.

Always finish your workout with sit-ups and stretching.

Tricep Kickback

Bend at the waist so that your upper body and upper arm are parallel to the floor. It helps to use a chair for support.

Move your arm only from below the elbow, and straighten out until it's fully extended. Keep your arm close to your side for the entire exercise.

Continue to use good form as you return the weight to the starting position.

Squats

Hold two dumbbells and stand with your feet a little wider than shoulder width.

Bend at the knees until your thighs are parallel to the floor (it's bad for your knees to bend lower than this). Keep your back straight and look forward when you bend.

Calf Raises

Hold two dumb-bells . . .

. . . and rise up onto your toes.

Leg Curls

You need a machine for this exercise.

Curl you legs until your calves are perpen-dicular to the floor.

Leg Extension

Again, you'll need to do this exercise on a machine.

Fully extend your legs.

For Hockey Players Only: A Wrist Exercise to Improve Your Shot

Tie a weight to a dowel (or hockey stick).

For a great wrist exercise, reel up the weight by rotating your wrists as fast as you can.

Make sure to use your wrists to wind the weight down as well as up. Don't let it slip. You'll feel this one.

ROLLER AND STREET HOCKEY

Roller hockey barely counts as crosstraining for ice hockey because the two are so similar. Again, the skills you develop on wheels will be used on the ice. In fairness to ice hockey, the roller game may not be quite as fast or as smooth, and ice-skating is a little more precise than in-line skating. However, great improvements in your game can be made with a little time on in-line skates.

Most of what you learn in roller hockey can be used on the ice.

Street hockey is another great way to work on stickhandling and shooting. If you play in shoes, remember to cut your stick shorter than your ice or roller hockey stick (because you're shorter with your skates off). It's very helpful to set up a target and practice shooting at it over and over. A regulation ice-hockey net is six feet wide by four feet high. Draw a net of these dimensions on a wall with chalk. Draw a six-inch square in each corner of your net. Practice shooting balls at the four squares (the corners) until you can hit all of the targets consistently. Don't forget to hit all the squares with back-handed shots too.

Set up a "net" and practice shooting for the corners.

SWIMMING AND BIKING

Swimming and biking are two other great low-impact sports that can work both your aerobic and anaerobic systems. You can base workouts in these sports on the in-line skating workouts. Also, swimming is one of the few total-body exercises. It works both the upper and lower body equally.

STRETCHING

Flexibility is the key to a long athletic career and is very important for preventing and rehabilitating injuries. Never try to stretch when you're "cold." Heat up your muscles a bit by doing 10 to 15 minutes

Always stretch after a workout.

of exercise at a moderate pace, then stretch before your workout. Also, thoroughly stretching after the workout (after practice, after weight lifting, etc.) is very important. During the workout your muscles will be continuously contracting and will accumulate lactic acid. Stretching afterward returns pliability and can help remove lactic acid. Save long stretching routines for after your workout.

TIME OFF

Sorry, but it's true: you'll have to take some time off from hockey and training every season. Giving your muscles and mind a complete break is often the key to coming back at a higher level and rejuvenating your game. At the end of the season your body needs a break from all the work it's been doing, and it needs to make repairs. If you ever feel sluggish and things aren't "clicking" on the ice during the season, take a day or two off and you'll probably return with the intensity you've always had.

Women's Hockey Resources

THE INTERNET

The Internet is one of the best places for women's hockey information. You can easily search for your favorite college teams, as well as teams representing cities and countries.

The Women's Hockey Web Page

This site (www.whockey.com) was created by women's hockey fanatic Andria Hunter, and it is now the official unofficial site for women's hockey on the web. There is a link to just about every other women's hockey site in the world here, and the page receives thousands of hits a day.

Among other things, you can find information on leagues, rules, administrators, registered organizations, tournaments, camps, and events, and the sites for the national governing bodies of hockey in many countries of the world.

You can also get information about books and magazines dealing with women's hockey. I recommend you get to know this literature. Magazines cover the latest in women's ice and roller hockey and often feature international events and players. Magazines are also a great source of interviews, player and team profiles, equipment reviews, and tournament listings. Books are a great way to learn about women's hockey history, the struggles on the road to equality, and the accomplishments of other players and teams.

HOCKEY CAMPS AND INSTRUCTIONAL SCHOOLS

Attending a hockey camp is one of the fastest ways to make substantial improvements in your skills and understanding of the game. You will usually have three to four hours of time on the ice per day at a one- or two-week camp. Camp information is available at the women's hockey web page and in most hockey magazines and newspapers.

TOURNAMENTS

Tournaments are a great way to focus exclusively on hockey for the weekend and to play against teams from outside your area. There are thousands of tournaments each year; check the Internet for information. Females from around the world can still showcase their skills each year during one of the oldest surviving women's hockey traditions: the Brampton Canadettes Ladies Dominion Hockey Tournament. Not only has it been held since 1967, it is now the world's largest hockey tournament (male or female). Originally started at a single rink in Brampton, a suburb of Toronto, for a small group of local female players, the tournament inspired many girls from the area to start playing hockey, and outside teams wanted to compete against them. The tournament grew quickly.

Now, the Canadettes take over ten local skating venues for the weekend. They have to, in order to accommodate the 6,000 women and girls on 394 teams from around the world who make the trip to play in their tournament. Most national-team and college players have skated there. If you want to skate in front of college scouts, this is the place to be. Don't be intimidated, though; there are over 38 different divisions that accommodate all age and skill levels. I highly recommend this tournament, which is held on Easter weekend each year. It's organized and run very well—and is a lot of fun.

The New Jersey Colonials after winning a tournament.

INDEX